ENERGY

Anna Skowrońska

Graphic design and illustrations by
Agata Dudek and Małgorzata Nowak

Translation by Antonia Lloyd-Jones

Boxer Books

Every day, rivers flow; plants grow; birds twitter; and people work, play, and do a lot of thinking. This capacity for activity is called **energy**. Its name comes from the Greek language, in which *energeia* means "activity" or "action." There are various kinds of energy that come from a variety of sources. Energy can be stored and used in many ways. Nothing can happen without it, and no one can live without it. Although sometimes we might think it has run out, it never actually disappears, but just changes form.

THE BEGINNING

In the beginning, the universe was probably focused on a single point. It possessed unimaginable energy and density. Around 14 billion years ago, it began to expand and at the same time it slowly cooled. Eventually, the first atoms of helium and hydrogen were formed, and then the first stars, galaxies, and planets. Scientists believe that was how our universe came into being. It is still expanding and still possesses the same total energy as it did at the start.

Our planet was formed about four billion years ago out of dust and gases whirling around the Sun, and the Sun is its main source of energy.

NUCLEI OF
HELIUM
HEAVIER
ELEMENTS
THE BIG BANG
SMALL
GALAXIES
THE SOLAR SYSTEM
AND THE BIRTH OF LIFE

SOME FORMS OF ENERGY

Heat

When you heat water in a pot, the flame from the burner transmits energy to the water particles. They start to vibrate more and more intensely, until they pull away from one another and rise. That's when you see steam, which means the water is boiling. You must be careful not to burn yourself. Heat is the energy of the particles moving within a substance. The hotter it gets, the faster they move!

Sound

Whether you shout or talk in a whisper, your vocal cords move or vibrate and make the air around them move, too. Their energy is transmitted with the help of waves. It reaches our ears and makes our eardrums vibrate as well. That's how we hear sounds, like whispers and shouts!

Motion

You can only fly a kite when the wind is blowing. The energy of the moving air, or wind, makes the kite rise. And you can steer it using the string.

Resilience

When you pull back a bow, you store energy within it. When you let go, this energy is transmitted to the arrow, which makes it fly with great speed. In the same way, energy is stored in a tensed rubber band, gas under pressure, or a tightly coiled spring.
In the past, various machines, such as watches or music boxes, worked thanks to springs you had to wind up. There were even wind-up calculators!

Nutrition

All foods contain a store of **chemical energy**, which your body transforms into energy for activity. You think, read, play football, breathe, and grow. Everything, whatever your body does, happens thanks to energy. It is produced in the process of cellular respiration.

HOW TO GET YOUR FILL OF THE SUN

or how light energy changes into chemical energy

Animals and people get their food from other animals or plants, but what do plants eat? They obtain water from the soil and carbon dioxide from the air. This process only takes place in the presence of light. A green dye—we call it chlorophyll—absorbs light, which carries solar energy. Then a whole chain of events is set in motion. Plants use sunlight to help them turn water and carbon dioxide into food, called glucose, and release oxygen into the air. This entire operation is called **photosynthesis**. Its name comes from Greek, where *phos* means light and *synthesis* means something coming together. Energy is stored in glucose. Plants use glucose to grow, and it can be used for other purposes as well, including to transport water and mineral salts. And so, by eating plants, both humans and animals make use of this energy.

Light

The Sun sends us energy nonstop in the form of light, which moves at immense speed. It travels more than 93 million miles in approximately eight minutes! Nothing is faster than light. The vectors for solar energy are particles known as **photons**, which are particles of light.

The Sun vitamin

Vitamin D3 is produced in the human body with the help of sunlight. It is extremely important to our bodies. It helps us have greater immunity to various illnesses and stronger bones. In autumn and winter, when there is less sunlight, we should ingest it in the form of a supplement.

Electricity from algae

During photosynthesis, plants produce not just oxygen and carbohydrates but also electrons. Some British scientists have made use of this phenomenon to obtain electricity from the Sun and build a solar battery that contains algae. During the experiment, they used it to power a microprocessor for six months, and the battery still hadn't run out!

A solar snail

Snails usually move across leaves, but sometimes they simply look like leaves. ***Elysia chlorotica*** lives in the sea. Like other sea slugs, it eats algae. But unlike other sea slugs, it is able to use the chlorophyll it ingests along with the algae to nourish itself!

OUR MINI POWER STATIONS

The cells in our bodies have their own energy "generators." To find out how they work, first you must eat something.

When you sit down to breakfast, you can see the cornflakes, milk, and croissants, but you cannot see the carbohydrates, fats, and protein that form them. They are made of many elements, like a complicated toy-brick construction. In this form they won't fit in the cells of our body. They must be broken down into simpler parts.

Digestive juices are fluids that help to break down carbohydrates, fats, and protein into smaller particles.

Hydrochloric acid, which is secreted in the stomach, is highly caustic. If we were to pour some on our hands, it would burn us. But the stomach protects itself with special membranes. The acid disinfects food and helps us to digest it.

A journey among enzymes

When our breakfast is chewed and mixed with saliva, it changes into easy-to-swallow pulp. When it reaches the stomach, muscles break it down further, mixing it and releasing digestive juices. Your breakfast goes on to be processed inside the intestines. Finally, it finds its way into the blood, and from there, first it goes into the liver, which filters out impurities. That is where carbohydrates, now broken down into simple sugars, are changed into glucose, which the blood then carries directly to the cells.

Our intestines are from 26 to 33 feet long. The walls of the small intestine are thickly coated in intestinal villi, which are small, thin projections. There are so many of them that we could make a large carpet out of them! It is through the villi that nutritional components find their way into the blood.

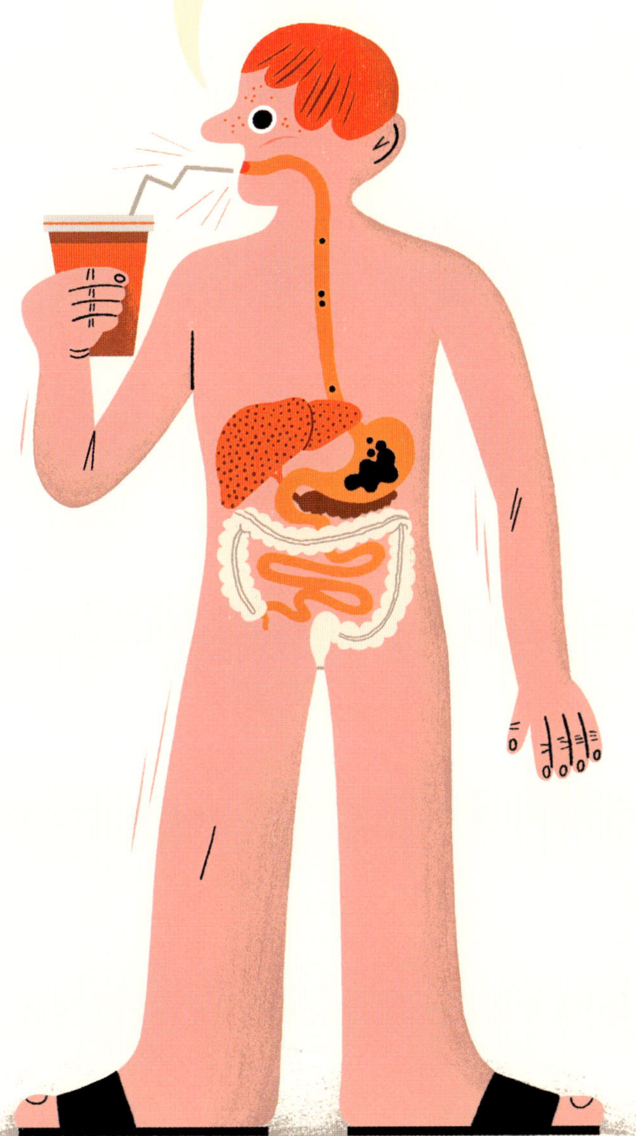

Batteries

Now the mitochondria—our personal "power stations"—come into play. They receive glucose, which, with the help of oxygen, they change into carbon dioxide and water. In the process, energy is released. The mitochondria store this energy in the form of particles known as **ATP**. Just as a mobile phone has a battery inside it, our body has ATP as its battery. It is our source of the energy we need to breathe, think, and move—in short, to live.

To function, our cells need glucose, just as a car needs gasoline.

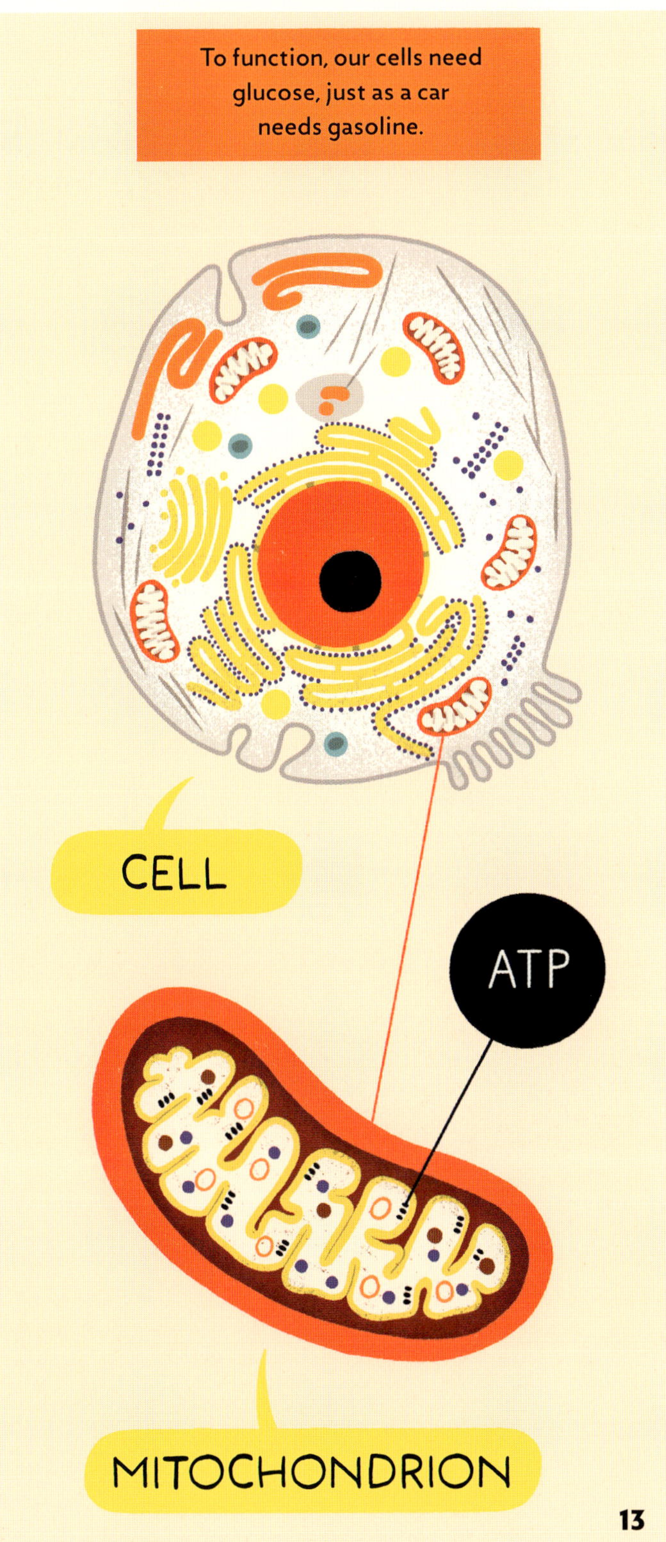

HOW MUCH ENERGY IS THERE IN A BANANA?

Everything we eat has its own **energy value**, meaning the amount of energy that is released while it is processed through our body. This is measured in **kilocalories** (kcal). Our breakfast, lunch, and dinner must provide us with the right amount of energy we are going to need while studying, playing, growing, and even sleeping. Not too much and not too little. What you eat matters—and so does how you eat it, so watch out! Being very full does not necessarily mean you are well nourished.

One calorie is roughly the amount of energy needed to raise one gram of water to one degree Celsius (1°C). In the past, it was a unit for measuring heat. **A kilocalorie is 1,000 calories**, but in everyday speech we refer to kilocalories as "calories."

When we say that one banana contains approximately 116 kilocalories, it means that if we eat it, it will provide us with roughly the amount of energy that we use during two hours of sleep.

WHAT SHOULD WE EAT?

Empty calories

Does a car move if you pour a carbonated drink into its tank? No. It is the same with our bodies. They won't "work" if we don't feed them properly. Except that a car without gas or electricity immediately stops working, while a badly nourished body only gives up after many years! Some food and drinks have a high energy value but no nutritional value. We call them empty calories. They include sugar, sweetened carbonated and noncarbonated drinks, chips, candy bars, candy, cookies, and so-called energy drinks. It's better to avoid them.

Check the labels on food products, and do not buy the ones that contain artificial coloring and lots of preservatives.

The **brain** is the command center for the entire body, and although it is not large, it uses a great deal of energy. **It likes to be well nourished**, as do the heart and other muscles.

HOW TO KEEP WARM

On a very hot day, we sweat because the water evaporating from our skin takes away energy and cools our body. This is our body's way of protecting itself against overheating. In turn, when the weather is very cold, it needs large amounts of energy to keep warm. Our bodies have mechanisms to maintain a stable internal temperature, and this uses energy.

During their expeditions, mountaineers spend a long time at extremely low temperatures. Even when they are not climbing, they are using the energy stored in their bodies, and they lose weight purely because of the cold! Dieticians work out special menus for them. They recommend high-calorie foods that can be eaten quickly and easily.

ANIMALS SAVE ENERGY

When the days become shorter, it gets cooler. The radiators come on in our houses, but in animals' burrows and hollows, there isn't any heat. Animals need to find a different way to **keep warm in winter**. They can sense that the time is approaching when they will have to protect themselves against the cold. Some migrate to warmer regions, change their diet, or go to sleep for months on end to save energy.

Slowly does it

In summer and early autumn, **bears** gorge themselves on food. They gain a layer of fat that will be their store of energy. In late December, they fall into a deep sleep and continue to sleep for several months. During this time, the rate of their breathing and heartbeat is reduced. This saves some of the energy stored in the fat. Even so, during their hibernation (as we call their winter sleep), they can lose as much as 440 pounds!

Bats hang head down in caves or old attics. They look as if they are dead, because they hardly breathe at all! They wake up every two or three months for various purposes, including to excrete waste. **Hedgehogs** roll up into a ball under leaves, and the rate of their heartbeat reduces from 180 to 20 beats per minute. During their hibernation, bats, hedgehogs, and bears reduce their body temperature to save energy on heating their body while they are asleep.

How do animals that do not hibernate find enough energy in winter?

Some animals, including storks and cranes, fly away to warm countries. Others eat seeds instead of insects. Some even change their fur in winter to stay warm. There are also animals that do not sleep but make use of a well-stocked pantry. In their homes, squirrels and mice store nuts, seeds, pine cones, fruits, and even mushrooms, which they eat in winter. In winter, beavers gorge on tree bark to give them energy through the cold winter months.

Foresters plant not just trees but also shrubs that provide food for birds and animals. Blackthorn, hawthorn, and spindle bushes are bird restaurants in winter.

Animals can store energy at other times of year, too. The camel's hump conserves energy in the form of fat. It makes use of this store during long and strenuous journeys.

HOW IS ENERGY CONVERTED?

We turn on the faucet, switch on the computer, or get into the car without giving it a second thought. Where does the hot water in the bathtub come from? How are we able to watch a match on the computer while it is being played on another continent? What makes the car go? Every one of these conveniences is the result of many years of work by all sorts of scientists, engineers, and inventors who have managed to harness the way **one form of energy changes into another**.

Striking fire

One of the most important discoveries to do with energy dates to prehistoric times, when human beings taught themselves how to kindle fire. It gave them heat and light and allowed them to cook food, fire clay, and smelt metals.

To set twigs alight, you must supply energy, by setting a lighted match to them, for example. If there is enough energy, the firewood heats up, and then the particles that form it will start to vibrate. They will move faster and faster, bumping into one another, pushing and shoving, until finally they combine with oxygen in the air. This starts a combustion reaction, which transforms the energy stored in the wood into heat. When the heat is great enough, some of the energy radiates as light.

WAYS TO KINDLE FIRE

Under the floor

On chilly days, the rich residents of ancient Rome liked to walk across heated floors. They laid the floors on stone pillars with empty space between them. At a central point underneath the floor, there was a furnace, and the fire burning in it heated the air between the pillars, which warmed the floor tiles. The world's oldest underfloor heating system, which existed in ancient Greece and Rome, is called a **hypocaust**.

Catching the wind

The wind's energy comes from the Sun, which heats the Earth more powerfully in some places than in others. Wherever it is hotter, the air takes on heat from the land or the ocean. It rises. Its particles move faster and faster, occupying more and more space. The air thins out, and we call that a depression. Meanwhile, in another place, where it is cool, the air is denser, and its particles are more crowded—we call that a high. When two of these regions are located next to each other, the particles naturally shift to where there is more space. The result is wind, which can be a powerful source of energy. The ancient Egyptians used it by sailing along the river Nile in boats with a single sail. Whereas the Persians and Chinese built windmills, whose sails were moved by the wind, setting machinery in motion for milling grain or draining the soil.

A fair wind to America

In 1492, Christopher Columbus set out on a voyage from the port of Palos in Spain. He sailed westward, believing he was going to find a new route to the land of spices—India. He set off with 90 sailors on three ships. On October 12, 1492, the energy of permanent winds carried them to an unfamiliar land. Coming to America brought great wealth to the Spanish, fame to Columbus, and persecution and suffering to the indigenous Native Americans.

There are places on Earth that permanently receive more energy from the Sun's rays and heat up the fastest, and others where less sunlight gets through. This constant difference in temperature over large areas causes winds that almost always blow in the same direction—we call them **permanent winds**.

Energy in the soil

In a single mug of earth we can find all sorts of living creatures, including bacteria, fungi, and other microorganisms too small to be seen with the naked eye. Yet they have an important task to perform. They are responsible for the decomposition of the remains of animals, plants, and waste matter. They process them into simple organic compounds, which then go back into plants with water as food, and therefore as energy. Microorganisms have been fertilizing the soil in this way for millions of years, long before people learned to cultivate plants and fertilize the fields.

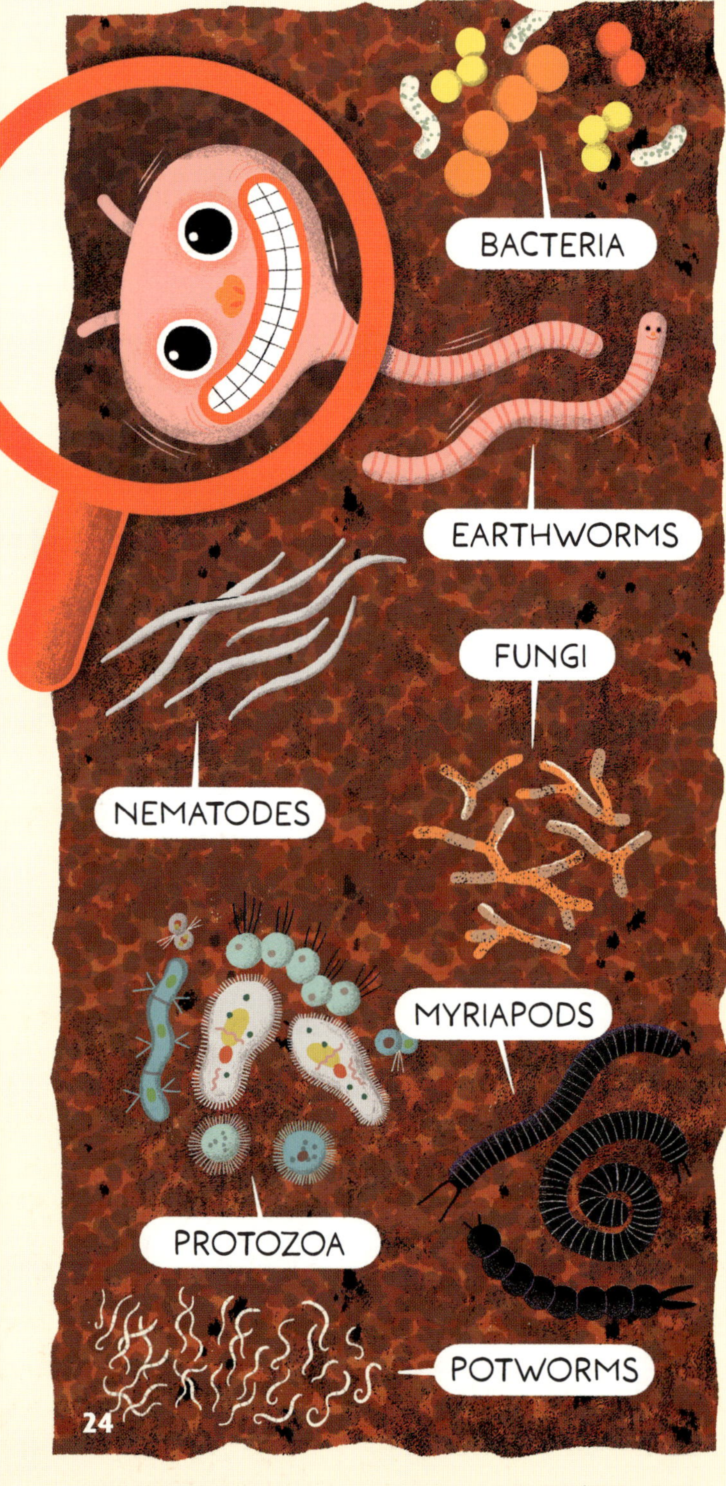

Zero waste from 2,000 years ago

Almost two thousand years before Columbus landed in America, the inhabitants of the Amazon rainforest fertilized the soil with ashes, waste matter, pieces of broken pottery, animal bones, and charcoal. They wasted nothing, and they created a thick layer of very fertile black soil, known today as *terra preta*. Amazingly, it has survived, and it has preserved its properties, even though nobody took care of it for hundreds of years, and the tropical rains of the Amazon jungle rapidly rinse nutritional substances out of the earth. Apparently, *terra preta* can regenerate, thanks to the microorganisms of which it is composed. Now scientists are trying to find a way to recreate this type of soil, because tropical rainforests could grow again in it.

Flour made with water

In ancient times, the first waterwheels were produced. They changed the energy of flowing water into rotary motion, which started up machinery inside mills for milling grain into flour. The wheels used in sawmills changed the energy of water into a swinging motion, which activated machinery that cut timber.

Pumping water into the palace

Every year, approximately 15 million tourists from all over the world visit the palace and gardens at Versailles, just outside Paris. But they can no longer see the water system that was built there 340 years ago. In those days, France's absolute monarch, King Louis XIV, wanted water to be brought to Versailles from the River Seine, 492 feet below. So he summoned Europe's best engineers to design a system that would make it possible. Rennequin Sualem, an engineer based in Liège in Belgium, designed a device that would harness the river's energy. This involved building a dam. The water gathered by the dam beat against 14 waterwheels (each with a diameter of 40 feet), which activated a system of pumps connected by chains. They pumped water from the Seine through cast-iron pipes to a nearby hill, where an aqueduct nearly 2,000 feet in length carried it to a tank in Versailles. It took the energy of 1,800 workmen four years to complete the complicated system. In due course, the royal gaze could enjoy the sight of 1,600 fountains, which consumed more water than the whole of Paris.

ENERGY CHANGES THE ECONOMY

A horse works like an ox

For centuries, horses were the equivalent of cars, trains, and agricultural machines. They pulled carts, coaches, and sleds. They transported people and goods. They delivered the post. Harnessed to plows, they worked in the fields, and also turned treadmills. The work that is now done by machines previously relied on the energy of a horse's muscles. In a treadmill, the animals walked around in a circle for several hours, turning a wheel that activated the drive for a piece of machinery. In mines, this system was used to bring salt or coal up to the surface and to send the miners underground. In villages, it was used to thresh grain. In some parts of the world treadmills were turned by oxen, donkeys, and even people.

TREADMILL

The "engine" has a rest

In 1866, Warsaw's first tram departed from Inżynierska ("Engineer's") Street and ran from Wilno Station to a station at the junction of Marszałkowska Street and Jerozolimskie Avenue. Each of the red cars weighed more than two tons and could carry 35 passengers and their luggage. They ran along a track which occasionally branched off to allow the trams to pass each other. They were pulled by two horses, driven by a coachman. At the end of the route the horses had a rest.

Hands to work

Not just animals worked in the fields or mines. In various parts of the world the hard labor was done by people who were forced to do it. In Europe the fields were cultivated by serfs. These peasants were bound to a plot of land by the nobleman who owned it in exchange for certain obligations. Western Europe gradually gave up serfdom, while the eastern part of the continent made increasing use of it. The peasants often had to work seven days a week without pay. Their master could sell them, transfer, or pawn them. Russia was the last country to abolish serfdom, in 1861.

In the United States in the nineteenth century, "hands to work in the fields" were on sale at markets. Numerous advertisements praised the "goods," who were human beings. After being captured in Africa or Central America, these enslaved people were sold to cotton plantations in the Deep South of the Unites States. There they worked from dawn to dusk, without any pay and without any rights.

According to the historian Alessandro Stanziani, until the mid-nineteenth century most of the energy used in farming relied on the physical labor of people and animals. It was only the industrial revolution and machines that brought change.

The engine that accelerated a revolution

When the fashion for cotton fabrics was at its height in England, merchants started bringing them all the way from Asia. The English clothmakers did not like this. Afraid that their own products would cease to sell, they brought about a ban on the import of these fabrics. This prompted the merchants to import raw cotton from Asia instead. Straight off the plant, cotton looks like white wool, and at first they found it hard to produce cloth with it. Someone had to make yarn out of it and then use the yarn to make material. The existing workshops were too small and too slow to keep up with the orders. So, larger factories were established, where increasingly modern machinery was used. At exactly this time, 29-year-old James Watt constructed the first fully developed **steam engine**.

Watt did not have the money to manufacture lots of engines. He made a deal with Matthew Boulton, who bought the patent from him, and they began working together. By the start of the nineteenth century, they had made 250 engines, which were immediately put to use at spinning mills, in agriculture, and in mines. Thanks to one of these engines, a factory could produce more yarn or fabric at a faster rate.

Production got moving, literally at full steam. Now all that was missing was the transport to fetch coal and distribute the goods. Until now, horses had been the main means of pulling the carts, carriages, or barges that traveled along rivers. Now steam locomotives and steamships appeared.

Within a steam engine a whole series of transformations of energy takes place. First the energy stored in coal when it is burned changes into heat, which heats a boiler filled with water. The water boils, producing steam, and in the process increases its volume. It is compressed inside the boiler. Have you ever seen the lid on a pot of boiling water jumping up and down? That is the result of compressed steam trying to escape its confinement. The same thing happens inside a steam engine, except that instead of rattling a lid, the steam moves pistons. And then the pistons activate a machine. A steam turbine works in a similar way, except that instead of pistons it has turbines—wheels with paddles, a bit like mill wheels. This design is used to the present day at the biggest, most modern power stations. But the system has been perfected and does not necessarily use coal to heat the water.

Horses in a locomotive
In the eighteenth century, horses were harnessed to special devices to activate machines. Watt's engine was far more efficient. Wanting to advertise it, Watt defined its power in terms of . . . horses! Doing the same work as a horse, a steam engine had the power of three mechanical horses. Why three and not one? Because a horse worked for eight hours a day, but the engine could work for 24 hours a day—in other words, three times longer. To this day the power of engines is defined in terms of mechanical horses!

The rocket

These days rockets fly to the Moon, or even Mars. Modern trains can reach a speed of more than 250 miles per hour. "Rocket," the locomotive designed by Robert Stephenson, "tore along the tracks" at a speed of 30 miles per hour, but in 1829, that was seen as phenomenally fast. Several tons of coal had to be taken on board to keep fueling the boiler. The boiler heated water, the water turned to steam, and the steam set the wheels in motion.

This sort of locomotive was too heavy to move along ordinary roads. Solid iron tracks were needed. The construction of the railway network began—first in the United Kingdom, then in Belgium, Germany, and France.

FIRST COSMIC SPEED - 4.9 M/S

STEPHENSON'S ROCKET,
SPEED - 30 MPH

In 1825, the first passenger train ran from Stockton to Darlington in England. It had an average speed of 8 miles per hour, and was greeted at the station by crowds of curious onlookers.

The Liverpool to Manchester railway line transported people and goods. Its opening in 1830 was such a major event that it was commemorated on souvenir mugs and bowls!

The Chinese train Shanghai Transrapid can travel as fast as 373 miles per hour. In Europe, the fastest train is the French TGV. Its record speed is 356 miles per hour.

Horses in retirement

In the past, horses pulled carts carrying coal from the mines. They ran along wooden tracks. When locomotives appeared, the British satirists drew pictures of horses that had lost their jobs, and now had to earn a living playing in an orchestra.

COAL

To produce cotton fabrics and other items, modern machines were needed, and to make them steel was required—steel that was smelted in furnaces which were powered by coal. At first, charcoal (wood coal) was used. But over time, as more and more steelworks were established, there wasn't enough wood. There was a shift to using **hard bituminous coal**, which additionally provided far more energy. The coal was distributed by trains, powered by coal. The chain of needs began and ended with coal, and as a result it soon became the **king of energy**. It heated private homes and furnaces for smelting steel, activated the machines at factories, and powered ships and locomotives. It was not until the mid-twentieth century that coal was partly deposed by oil and gas.

A king of moss and fern

If you were to bury plants in the earth and wait for coal to be formed out of them, it would be of no use, because you would have to wait millions of years. Approximately 300 million years ago, mosses and ferns were taller than many of today's pine trees. They grew on boggy ground. When they died, they sank into the marshy soil. Over time, they sank deeper and deeper. Their remains underwent compression, and as a result of high temperatures and pressure, they gradually changed into rock, the main component of which is coal. The solar energy that nourished the prehistoric plants is stored within it and can be released by burning. The resulting products are heat and light.

Coal is formed over millions of years. Its deposits are not renewable and their quantity is limited.

GAS

When you brush your teeth in the morning, you probably don't stop to wonder where the hot water comes from. Meanwhile, it may well be heated by a gas boiler. Natural gas was formed millions of years ago from the remains of animals and plants. Deposits of gas are found deep below the surface of the Earth, and inside cracks and gaps in rocks. To extract it, sometimes it is necessary to drill almost a mile underground. Gas reaches our homes through pipes. It is the fuel that heats the water in a central heating system and the water we use for bathing.

The United States produces nearly all of the natural gas that it uses from its own reserves.

In the past, the water for bathing was heated in two tanks. Sometimes it ran out in the middle of your bath and you had to finish it with cold water. On other occasions, only a little of it was used, and some of the energy was wasted. The German engineer Hugo Junkers found a solution. He constructed a gas boiler that heated water flowing through a system of pipes straight to the tap. Thanks to this, he obtained exactly as much hot water as he needed at the time, no more or less. His invention saved energy! To this day, Junkers's boilers heat the water in bathrooms.

Urban coal-gas lighting

Before darkness falls, in the oldest district of the Polish city of Wrocław the lamplighter appears. He carries a long pole, which he uses to light the gas lamps. It takes him nearly an hour, because there are almost 100 of them! At daybreak, as it becomes light, he returns to walk more than two miles again to put out the lamps. These days the lamps are just a tourist attraction, but there was a time when they were the most modern form of lighting.

In the days when Europe's lamplighters lit the street lamps each evening, the lights were fueled by gas derived from coal. This was the invention of William Murdoch, a Scottish engineer who heated coal to a very high temperature in an airtight oven, called a retort. Deprived of oxygen, the raw material did not burn, but gave off gas. Murdoch set a match to the retort's outlet and saw that it burned with a beautiful, bright flame. Soon he had constructed lamps, which he supplied with gas through pipes that ran straight from the retort, and lit the interior of his house. The year was 1792, and the discovery of coal gas entirely changed city life. Gas lamps were soon lighting the streets of London, Berlin, Paris, and Warsaw.

Urban gasworks were established, where underneath the airtight chamber of a retort filled with coal there was a hearth. The temperature went up to 1,200 degrees, and the resulting gas was distributed through pipes to the city's lamps and houses.

The first urban gasworks was built in London in 1812.

In the course of the twentieth century the use of urban gas gradually declined. It was replaced by natural gas and electricity.

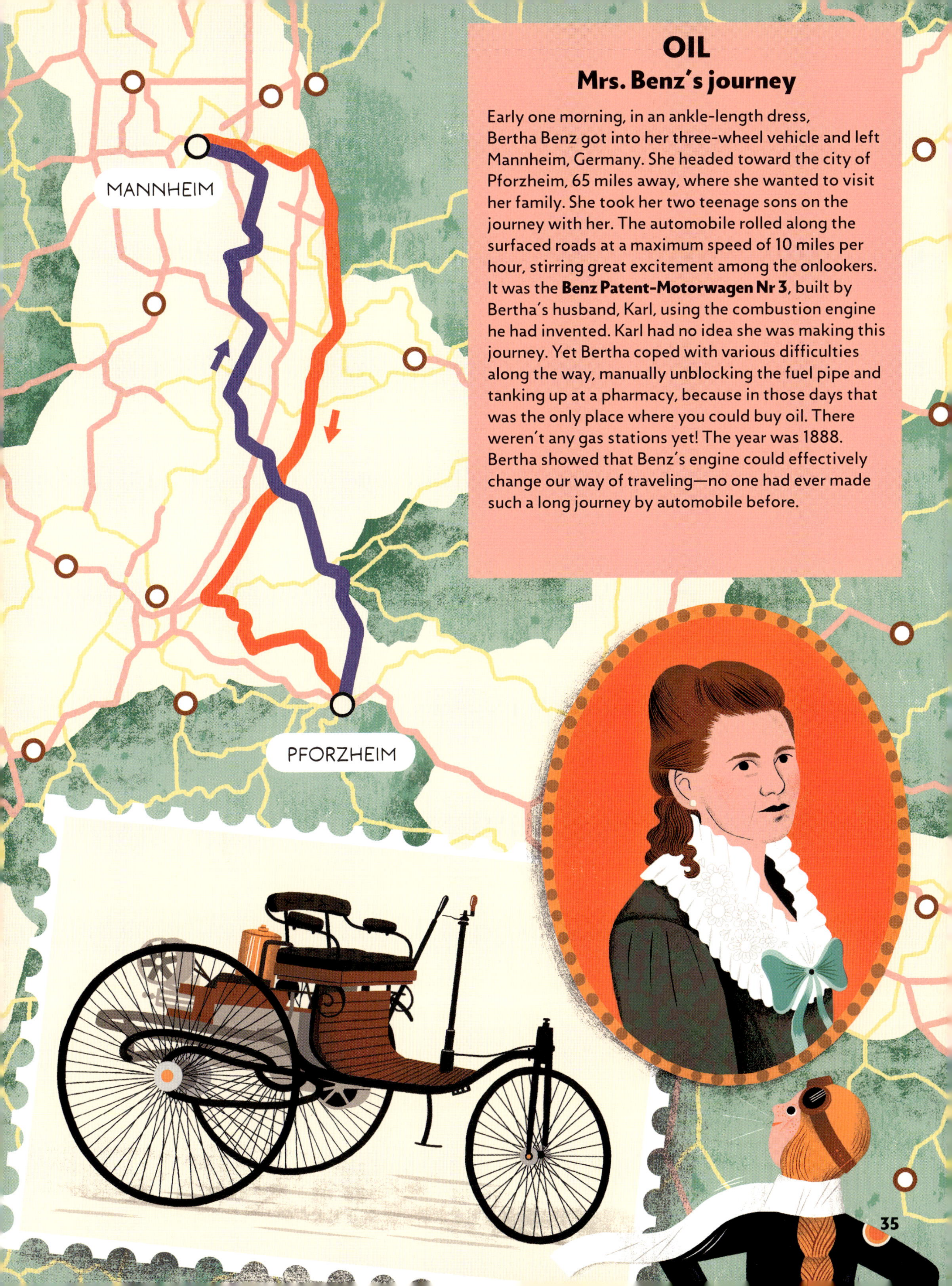

OIL

Mrs. Benz's journey

Early one morning, in an ankle-length dress, Bertha Benz got into her three-wheel vehicle and left Mannheim, Germany. She headed toward the city of Pforzheim, 65 miles away, where she wanted to visit her family. She took her two teenage sons on the journey with her. The automobile rolled along the surfaced roads at a maximum speed of 10 miles per hour, stirring great excitement among the onlookers. It was the **Benz Patent-Motorwagen Nr 3**, built by Bertha's husband, Karl, using the combustion engine he had invented. Karl had no idea she was making this journey. Yet Bertha coped with various difficulties along the way, manually unblocking the fuel pipe and tanking up at a pharmacy, because in those days that was the only place where you could buy oil. There weren't any gas stations yet! The year was 1888. Bertha showed that Benz's engine could effectively change our way of traveling—no one had ever made such a long journey by automobile before.

Cars

The first cars looked a bit like horse-drawn carriages, but instead of horses, they were "pulled" by an engine. Today, there are millions of cars all over the world, they fill up with fuel at gas stations, straight into the tank, and no one would think of limiting the speed to 10 miles per hour.

At the heart of a car is its engine, powered by **gasoline** or **diesel**, the fuel that provides the energy needed for driving. Both of these kinds of fuel are the products of **crude oil**, mined from underground. This raw material is formed from the remains of animals and plants that lived millions of years ago, and one day we will run out of it. While it is burning, harmful substances are produced, which, despite better and better engines and filters, pollute the environment.

The world's biggest producers of oil are the United States and Saudi Arabia.

The first vehicles powered by electricity appeared about 50 years before Mrs. Benz set off on her journey. But at the time, this type of transport did not catch on! Combustion engines won the hearts of drivers, and conquered the market. You could only play with a battery-powered car as a children's toy. Today we see them on the roads more and more often. These cars do not emit exhaust fumes and are very quiet. They have electric engines that draw an electric current from a set of accumulators. Instead of filling up, the driver must recharge the car like a cell phone. However, while you can charge a mobile phone anywhere, you can only charge a car at a special site. In many countries, there is no network of stations to provide the cars with energy yet. Maybe one day, charging stations will be as common as gas stations.

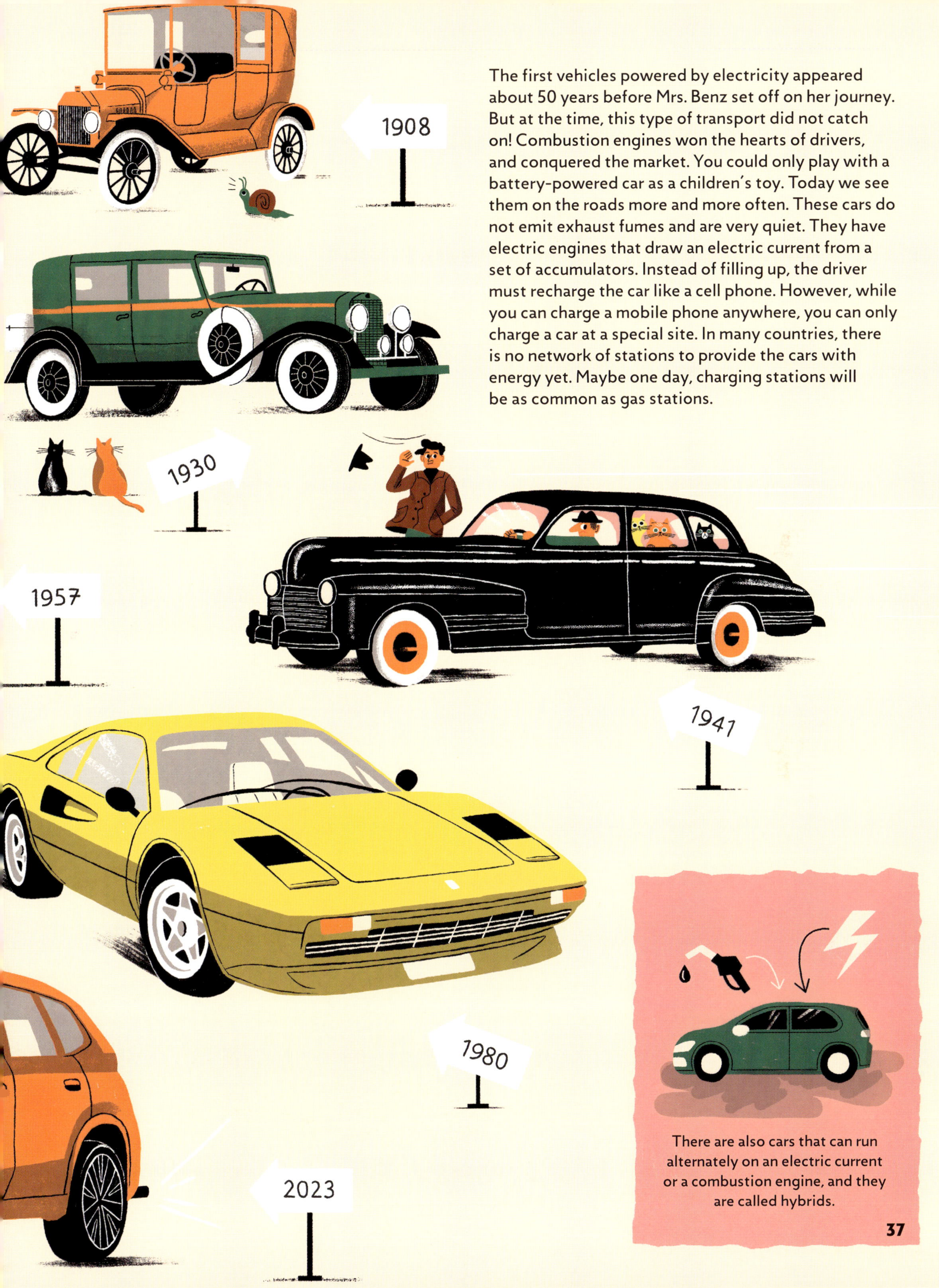

There are also cars that can run alternately on an electric current or a combustion engine, and they are called hybrids.

ELECTRICITY

In the past, you would have used an abacus instead of a calculator, a broom instead of a vacuum cleaner, and a washtub instead of a washing machine. To fetch milk, you had to go down to the cellar, which served as a refrigerator, and you could only listen to music if it was played live. There weren't any movies at all. Later on, electricity appeared, and it changed everything!

First, it lit up interiors in a completely unfamiliar way. Electric lamps didn't produce soot, or make it necessary to ventilate the rooms or keep cleaning soot off the lampshades. The light was definitely brighter and didn't flicker.

The lamps were followed by many appliances that made life easier. Some of them were already familiar but had only ever been used manually, such as coffee grinders, meat grinders, or juice squeezers, requiring time and effort. Their electrical equivalents made cooking easier and faster. Appliances such as vacuum cleaners, refrigerators, and washing machines genuinely revolutionized the lives of homeowners.

Energy behind the walls

When you switch on a computer or a light or dry your hair, you use electricity. Hidden behind the walls in our homes, there is a whole network of wires that carry electricity to the plug sockets and switches. And sometimes it comes from power stations that are far away. At those power stations, turbines activate a generator that processes the energy produced by their motion into electrical energy. High-tension cables deployed all over the country deliver the electricity to cities and towns, and then directly to schools, sports arenas, shops, movie theaters, and houses.

At a conventional power station, the turbines are activated by steam that is heated by coal, gas, or oil.

We cannot see electricity, just as we cannot see the wind. We only perceive its effects when a light bulb shines or the washing machine works. An electric current is the organized movement of electrons that carry energy.

Elektron is the Greek word for amber. The ancient Greeks noticed that when you rub amber against cloth, it attracts very small, light objects—it is electrified. But these experiments did not lead to any inventions. Today, we use the word *electron* to describe a tiny particle that has a negative electric charge.

IS THE EARTH TOO HOT?

You have probably run outside on a cold day without your hat and scarf and regretted it. You were freezing! Another time, your parents made you wear a hood on top of your hat and you felt too hot. To make sure we do not freeze or overheat, we have to dress the right way. Our planet has a well-organized system for protecting itself against losing heat and against overheating. Unfortunately, we have caused some confusion. Our Earth's hat and scarf is the atmosphere. Among other things, it is made up of greenhouse gases, which make sure it is warm enough for us. Without them, the planet would be covered in ice. But if there are too many of these gases, the Earth feels as if someone has put a hat on its head, a hood on top of that, and also wrapped it in a scarf!

ATMOSPHERE

GREENHOUSE GASES

The Sun sends us energy in the form of photons, which pass through the atmosphere. Some of them reflect off clouds and the Earth's surface, and some are absorbed by earth, water, and air, heating them. The Earth also radiates its own heat into the cosmos. Greenhouse gases in the atmosphere stop some of this radiation and reflect it, so that it returns to the Earth's surface. The effect is similar to a greenhouse, where strawberries can ripen out of season.

Greenhouse gas

Carbon dioxide is the most familiar greenhouse gas. It performs the role of an insulator in the atmosphere. But if there's too much carbon dioxide, it's like having too many blankets—the Earth gets too hot. When we burn coal and oil, it sends more carbon dioxide into the atmosphere.

CYCLE OF COAL IN NATURE

CO_2

PHOTOSYNTHESIS

BREATHING

FOOD

DECOMPOSITION

BURNING FOSSIL FUELS

Coal is still the world's most commonly used raw material for producing electricity. Worldwide, 61% of the power stations are fueled by coal, gas, and oil.

As each person breathes, they inhale oxygen from the atmosphere and exhale carbon dioxide. Plants do the opposite: they take in carbon dioxide from the atmosphere and emit oxygen. This exchange does not cause an imbalance as long as there are enough large plants in the world. Carbon dioxide is made up of one carbon atom and two oxygen atoms, or CO_2 for short. *C* stands for carbon, and *O* for oxygen. You hear a lot about it because there is too much of it!

Satellites to help

If you look at the sky at night, as well as stars, you will see an increasing number of satellites. Some of them study the weather and the climate, allowing us to see how much CO_2 there is. But of course they don't work like gas detectors! They study the flow of solar rays that bounce off the Earth and go back into the cosmos. Physicists use data of this kind to determine whether the amount of CO_2 in the atmosphere is increasing.

CLEAN ENERGY

If we were to close all the coal-fueled power stations today, most of the world's cities would be plunged into darkness. Coal is still the basic source of electrical energy. But when it is burned, it releases substances into the atmosphere that are harmful to us and our planet. On top of that, the world's coal deposits are not unlimited. For several decades, the world's scientists have been looking for new sources of energy. At first, the driving force behind this search was fear that one day we would run out of coal, oil, and gas. Since then, the need to limit the warming of our planet from pollution has been the focus.

Electricity from the air

Centuries ago, wind moved the sails of windmills that set various mechanisms in motion. In China they were used to drain fields, in the Netherlands to pump water out of marshes, and in Poland and France most often to make flour. Sometimes they powered sawmills, or helped to extract olive oil. These days, very few old windmills still function, and most of them only exist as exhibits in open-air museums.

In various parts of world, on land and in the sea, completely new wind turbines are being built. They exploit the same source of energy as the old windmills, but now the wind hits enormous blades that activate a rotor connected to a generator. The generator transforms the mechanical energy into electricity. They are put up in groups, often spread over vast areas, but only where strong, permanent winds are blowing. Otherwise they would miss their purpose. This new form of power station is called a wind farm.

There is no place where the wind blows nonstop. Even if a wind farm is situated at the most advantageous location, there can always be interruptions. When this happens, we need electricity from other sources.

Kite power

Above the sea flies a swarm of large, brightly colored kites pulling kite surfers along. In the near future, kites like these may be used to activate electricity generators. Ideas are being developed to use kite-activated generators to power domestic turbines and even power stations.

Pros:

- Wind energy is renewable, so the resource never runs out.
- It doesn't harm the environment, but works in harmony with nature.

Cons:

- Land turbines take up a lot of space, spoil the landscape, and make noise.
- The best terrain for wind farms is often far from the large cities they are to supply with energy, which can mean a rise in the price of electricity, because it has to be transported a long way.
- Establishing wind farms in the sea is very expensive and takes a long time.

Some turbines are very tall—taller than the Statue of Liberty in the United States.

From the river's current to the electrical current

In many parts of the world, water helps to light the houses or power the computers. This is made possible by building power stations on rivers. Dams accumulate water which falls and activates turbines. The turbines create energy which powers generators that produce electricity. Dams make it possible to regulate the release of the water.

The biggest dam in the world is on a river in China called the Yangtze. The Three Gorges Dam is 607 feet high, more than 0.6 of a mile wide and more than 1.2 miles long. The electricity is produced by 34 generators.

Pros:

- Once constructed, a hydropower station is easy to use and does not pollute the environment.
- As long as the water is flowing, there will be electricity.

Cons:

- Building a dam involves flooding a vast area.
- Dams obstruct animals' migration routes.

The high and low tides of the ocean can also be used to produce electricity. The water rises and recedes every day, moving turbines that generate energy. The French, Irish, Canadians, and Koreans all make use of tidal hydropower stations.

From the Sun

Why don't you need to change the batteries in your calculator? Perhaps it is powered by solar panels. These are thin plates that change solar energy into electricity. They come in various sizes, from the little panels in your calculator to the kind you can place on the roof of your house, to enormous ones that serve as a source of power for the International Space Station.

Some solar-power stations are spectacular. At a location between Seville and Cordoba in Spain, 2,600 mirrors arranged in a circle reflect solar rays and focus them on a tall tower. The solar energy heats liquid salt, which in turn heats water. The steam that is produced moves turbines, which activate an electricity generator. This power station even generates electricity at night! In the course of a year it powers 30,000 houses.

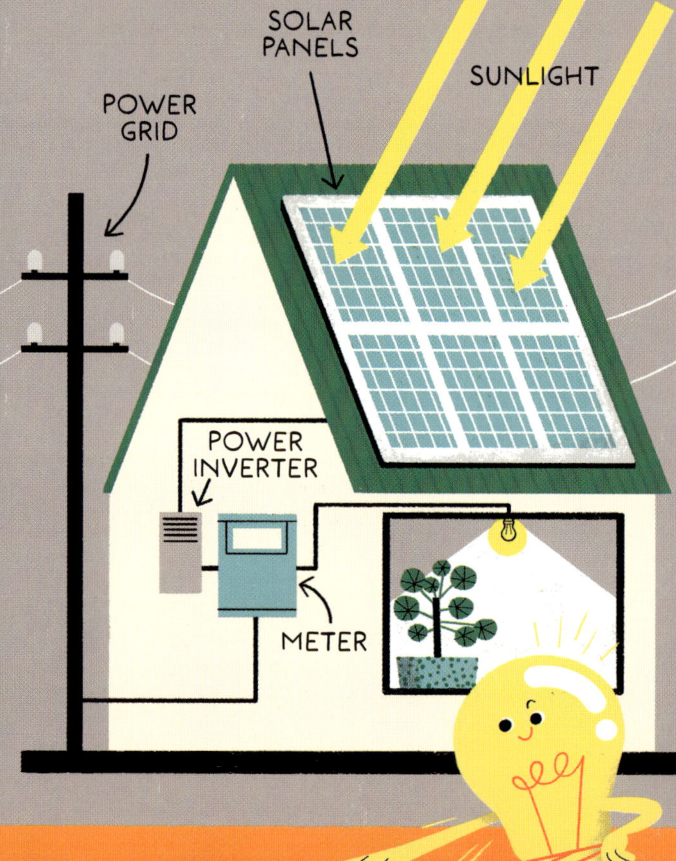

Pros:

- Using the natural movement of water does not harm the environment.

Cons:

- Tidal hydropower stations do not provide a huge amount of energy and they are expensive to build.

Pros:

- It does not pollute the environment.

Cons:

- It makes sense in places where there is a lot of sunlight. When there is none, there is no electricity either.
- It is still rather expensive.

From inside the Earth

At the very center of the Earth lies its **core**. It is spherical, and its outer part consists of fluid iron that is constantly in motion. Its temperature is almost as high as 8,500°F! The core is surrounded by the **mantle**, which is formed of partly molten, shifting masses of rock, or **magma**. On top of the mantle lies the thinnest layer, the **crust**. Heat from inside the Earth radiates to the outside. Magma heats rocks and underground waters.

To extract energy from the Earth's interior, two boreholes are made: one to pump cold water under the surface and a second to extract it, now heated. The hot water is piped directly to residential buildings, schools, swimming pools, etc. Once the water has given off its heat, it returns underground, where it heats up again. There are also places where water emerges from underground deposits of its own accord in the form of hot springs. This is the case in Iceland, where **geothermal energy** is commonly used.

EARTH'S ATMOSPHERE

CRUST

UPPER MANTLE

TRANSITION ZONE

LOWER MANTLE

OUTER CORE

INNER CORE

Pros:

- It is not dependent on the weather.
- It does not spoil the landscape.

Cons:

- It is only accessible in a few places.
- Sometimes the sources spontaneously disappear.

The deeper you go, the hotter it gets. The Earth's temperature increases on average by 72–87°F per mile.

FUSION POWER

TRITIUM DEUTERIUM

NEUTRON HELIUM

ENERGY

An artificial Sun

Have you ever wondered why the Sun shines? The source of its energy is **fusion**, meaning combination. The nuclei of hydrogen atoms combine with a helium nucleus, releasing vast energy in the process. Every second, within the core of the Sun, an unimaginable number of these fusions takes place.

What if we were to try to imitate the Sun and conduct a similar reaction on Earth? We would have clean, inexpensive energy. It sounds simple, but it is very difficult to do, because the nuclei of atoms repel each other, so first a vast amount of energy has to be used to combine them in order to gain even more energy. Within stars this happens in a natural way, because there are very high temperatures and immense pressure inside them. On Earth, first we would have to bring hydrogen to a temperature of about 200 million°F, making it change into a state of plasma. Only then will the nuclei approach each other. And then we would need to be able to repeat the reaction. Scientists and engineers in various countries have been working on this for more than 60 years.

If you like balloons, you probably know that they are most often filled with **helium**. This gas is lighter than air. That is why the balloons rise so easily.

Our Sun has a sufficient amount of hydrogen to shine for the next five billion years.

^{1}H PROTIUM

^{2}H DEUTERIUM

^{3}H TRITIUM

An **atom** is built of a nucleus and the **electrons** that move around it. The nucleus consists of **protons** and **neutrons**. Atoms of the same element that have the same number of protons and electrons but a different number of neutrons, are called **isotopes**. Deuterium and tritium are isotopes of hydrogen, or in other words they are variants of it. They are what is used for nuclear fusion. Deuterium is found in water, and tritium is sourced from rocks known as lithium. Their reserves are enormous.

Every second, the Sun changes 600 million tons of hydrogen into helium

15 to 20 kettles

In December 2022, while attempting fusion, several Californian scientists produced more energy than they used to bring about the reaction. But it didn't last very long. The resulting energy could not have lit up a city, but it could heat the water in 15-20 kettles. At a research laboratory near Oxford, England it has been possible to sustain fusion for as long as five seconds! Work on fusion is being conducted at several centers by scientists in Europe, America, and China.

A CHAIN REACTION

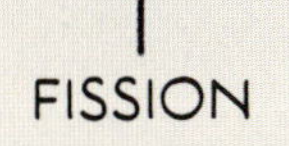

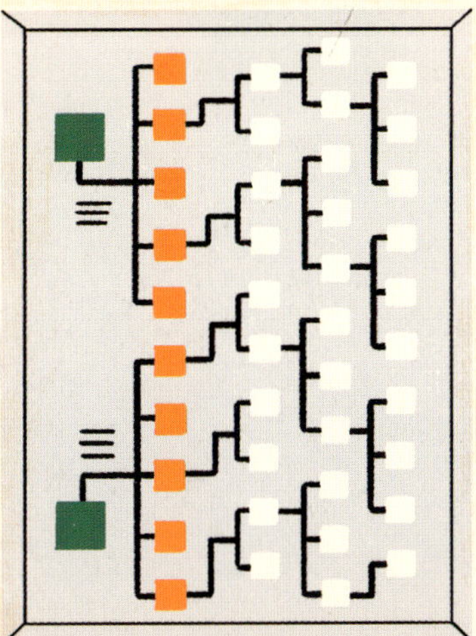

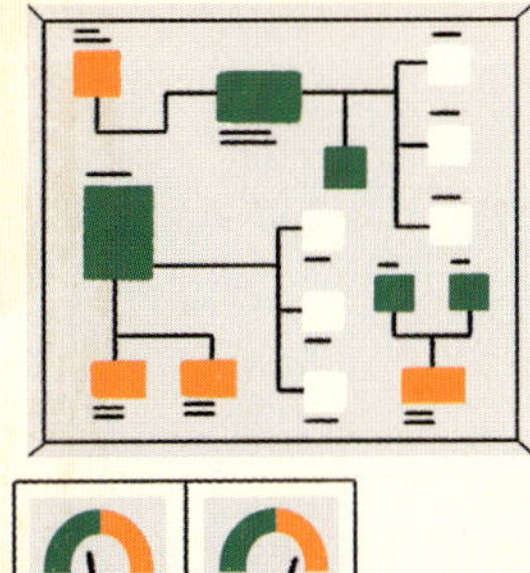

Pros:

- Fusion produces several million times more energy than burning fossil fuels.
- It is not a chain reaction, so in case of an accident, it does not present as great a danger as nuclear fission.
- The waste material is less radioactive than in nuclear fission.
- Deuterium and tritium are available in unlimited supply.

Cons:

- There are no power stations of this kind yet.

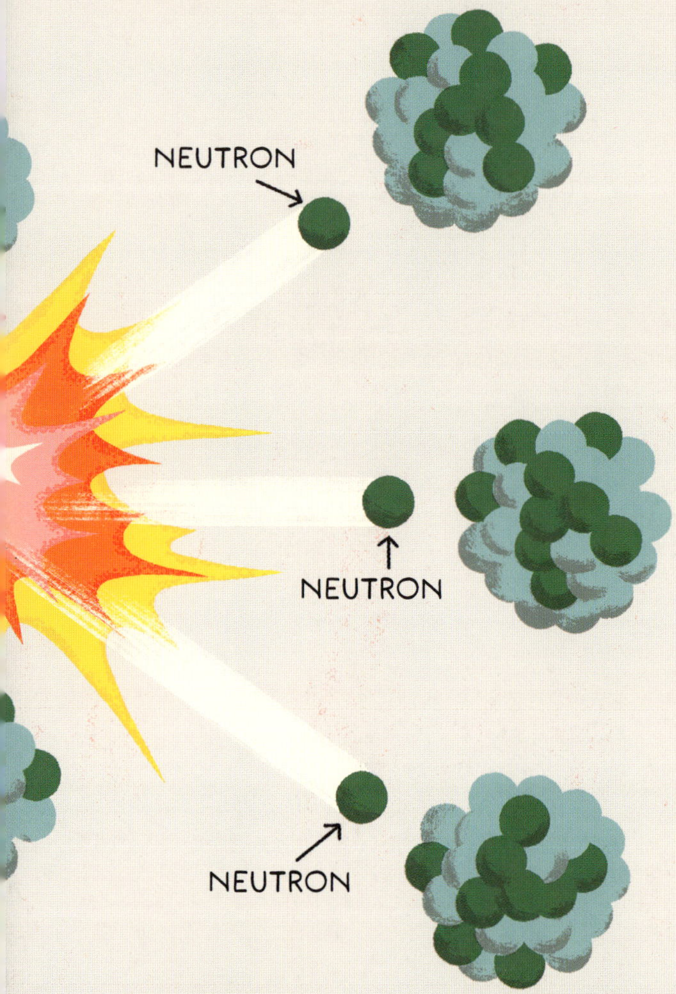

Fission

At the center of a nuclear power station is the reactor. Inside the reactor the nucleus of an atom is split in half, a process known as **fission**. This releases a large amount of energy, and at the same time, an eruption of neutrons occurs that causes further nuclei to divide. Once started, the process keeps spontaneously repeating. We call this a **chain reaction**. Within the reactor it is controlled to make sure it does not occur too quickly or too slowly.

In 2022, there were 239 power stations in operation worldwide. They are located in 32 countries. Another 60 are under construction. But what really matters is not how many of them there are, but how much electricity they produce.

NEUTRON

NEUTRON

NEUTRON

France has 56 reactors which provide up to 69% of the country's energy. Belgium has only 7, but they provide a little over half of the country's energy. In the United States 92 reactors provide 19.6%, while in China 55 reactors provide only 5%. Before the war in Ukraine, 55% of the country's energy came from 15 reactors.

The thermal energy released in the process of fission is transmitted to water. Then, as in a conventional power station, the resulting steam drives turbines, and a generator transforms their motion into electrical energy.

The main role in a nuclear power station is played by uranium, which is the fuel for the reactor. It is the atoms of uranium that are split. Uranium is mined from underground in the form of ore, a great deal of which is needed to obtain pure uranium. A ton of ore produces barely two pounds of pure uranium. But two pounds of uranium can be used to produce as much energy as 2,700 tons of coal!

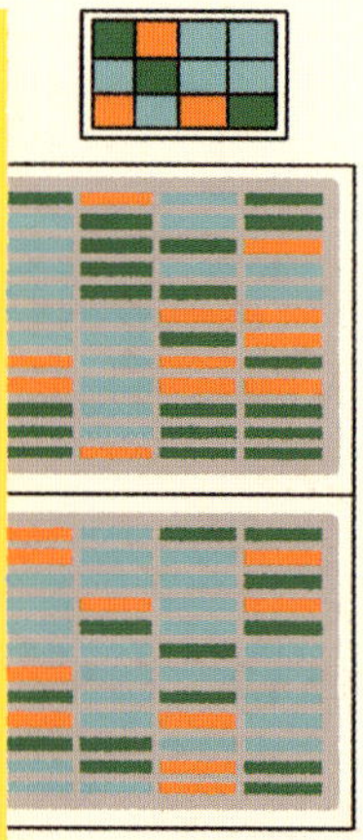

The most uranium ore is mined in Kazakhstan, Namibia, Canada, Australia, Uzbekistan, Russia, and Niger.

Pros:

- Nuclear power stations are highly productive.
- As long as there are no accidents, they do not pollute the environment.

Cons:

- During the fission of uranium, radioactive waste is produced, which is very dangerous for all living things. Unfortunately, it cannot simply be destroyed, because it will continue to emit harmful radiation. It has to be stored in special airtight containers. Luckily, there is not much of it relative to the energy produced.
- If an accident does happen, it can cause great radioactive contamination.

The power station in a sarcophagus

The greatest nuclear power station disaster ever took place at Chernobyl, then in the Soviet Union (now Ukraine). On the night of April 25 into April 26, 1986, the power-station employees were conducting an experiment designed to test the reactor's safety systems. But it went completely out of control. The reactor's power increased violently, which resulted in an explosion and then a fire. The firefighters were on the spot instantly. Unfortunately, they were not aware of the danger. They thought they were going to extinguish an ordinary fire. Large doses of radiation caused them to die. But the authorities tried to hush up the cause of the disaster. The next day, on April 27, everyone living in the neighboring area was evacuated, but they were still not told what had happened. Meanwhile, burning graphite rods were releasing strongly radioactive substances into the atmosphere. To stop this, the reactor was covered with sand and lead dropped by helicopters. But hot, radioactive air rose at rapid speed and was then driven by the wind in a northwesterly direction. The Soviet authorities did not inform anyone of the accident, although such a radioactive cloud was extremely dangerous for people's life and health. On April 28, when a Swedish survey noted a rise in radiation, and the media in the free countries began to publish information suggesting that a disaster may have occurred, the Soviet Union finally issued an official announcement. Several months after the disaster, the reactor was covered with a concrete coat, known as the sarcophagus, which does not let radiation through. Now the power station has been entirely decommissioned.

Radioactivity

Research into radioactive substances by Henri Becquerel, and then Marie Skłodowska-Curie and her husband, Pierre Curie, initiated the development of research into nuclear physics and chemistry.

After Chernobyl, the biggest nuclear power station disaster happened in Japan. In 2011, tsunami waves that were 50-feet high hit the shores of Japan, inundating the Fukushima power station. The reactors were instantly switched off when an earthquake was registered. But the tsunami waves damaged the power station's cooling system. The heat from the switched-off reactors was not drawn away, and three of the reactors' cores melted. The outcome of the accident was a hydrogen explosion.

Electricity in the toilet

You pee into a urinal, and it produces electricity. It sounds like a joke! And yet, in 2014, several British scientists based in Bristol elaborated this method and constructed a prototype of a urinal that uses urine to generate electricity. A year later, at the major Glastonbury music festival, toilets of this kind appeared. These urinals charge cell phones and power the lighting in the cabins! It is called "Pee-Power."

SAVING ENERGY

Toys, bananas, apples, shoes, dresses, T-shirts, and many other products use energy during production, and afterward, too, as they are supplied to our homes or shops. Even the potatoes or carrots that are grown near where we live have to be transported somehow. It is hard to imagine suddenly ceasing to produce, buy, or import goods, no longer traveling, and above all, not eating . . . but we can always try not to waste what we have and not to buy things we do not need.

Other methods of saving energy

Are you sitting at the table? Only put on your plate as much as you will eat. You can always add more.

Are you making tea? Only put as much water as you need in the kettle.

Are you leaving the kitchen? Switch off the light.

You're not charging your phone? Unplug the charger from the socket.

Are you going somewhere? Instead of going by car, go on foot, ride a bike, or use public transport.

On every electrical appliance you'll find a colored label. It tells you how much energy the object uses. This allows us to check which toaster will make delicious toast quickly using less electricity and which one uses more. Energy-saving light bulbs, refrigerators, washing machines, and kettles use up less energy. So they are more ecological, and we have lower electricity bills!

Never throw away batteries, used telephones, or other electrical appliances in an ordinary trash can. In most residential areas there are special containers for these items. Old refrigerators, batteries, broken fluorescent bulbs, or monitors contain various toxic or carcinogenic substances. If these fluids leak out, they get into the soil, and, from there, into the ground water.

BOXER BOOKS Ltd. and the distinctive Boxer Books logo are trademarks of Union Square & Co., LLC.
Union Square & Co., LLC, is a subsidiary of Sterling Publishing Co., Inc.

Originally published as *Energia* by Muchomor, Warsaw, 2023

English translation rights arranged through KaBooks rights agency – Karolina Jaszecka

This edition first published in North America in 2025 by Boxer Books Limited.

ISBN 978-1-4547-1269-5

For information about custom editions, special sales, and premium purchases, please contact specialsales@unionsquareandco.com.

Printed in China

Lot #:
10 9 8 7 6 5 4 3 2 1

04/25

unionsquareandco.com